Have You Ever Seen...?

An American Sign Language (ASL)
HANDSHAPE DVD/Book

Adonia K. Smith

E. Lynn Jacobowitz

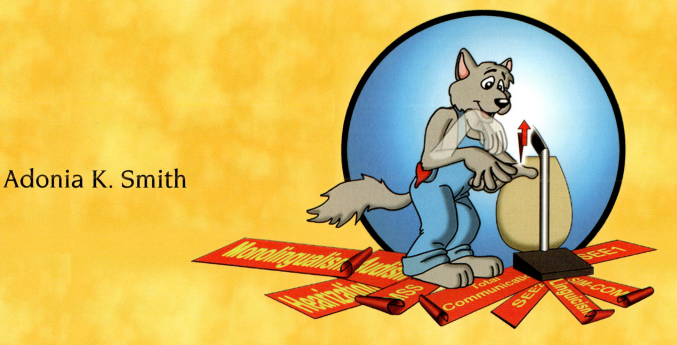

www.aslrose.com

Illustrated by Tamara Davidson
Video Directed by James R. DeBee
Cultural Vignettes Signed in ASL by Rosa Lee Gallimore
Signed in ASL by Deaf Children and KODAs of MD and TX

Dedication

To ASL/English bilinguals of K-12

Contents

Acknowledgments

Bringing to fruition the *Have You Ever Seen…?: An American Sign Language* (ASL) *Handshape* DVD/*Book* project has been a long, mind-boggling and exciting process that could not have succeeded without the assistance and support of many professionals, families and friends. We could not have accomplished this project without the educational insight, undying patience, endless time, and loving support of so many.

Since implementing this project, we have learned many things as the result of our interaction with people in this endeavor who gave us the opportunity to expand, investigate, and verify the way things are and the way they can be.

First, we wish to thank the special people in our project whose expertise, patience, and support have made this accomplishment possible:

Our families, Smith and Jacobowitz, for their love and encouragement to complete this project. They provided dependable, enthusiastic and ongoing support, both in person and in e-mails. We want to thank each individual member of both families. The Smith family members are Jesse (belated and beloved father), Nellie (mom), Camille Smith Whitfield (sister), David Whitfield (brother-in-law), Griffin and Andrew Whitfield (nephews). The Jacobowitz family members are Abraham Harry (father), Miriam (mother), Sheldon (brother), Tina (sister), Nicholas Michelli (brother-in-law), Kathleen M. Wood (lifelong partner), Eve and Anna (daughters).

Dr. Lawrence Fleischer, chair of the Deaf Studies Department at California State University at Northridge, for providing cultural information and insight of how best to gear this project to particular audiences.

Dr. Eddy Laird, professor at McDaniel College, for creating the introduction of this project and sharing his expertise in first language acquisition.

Dr. Ceil Lucas, professor in the Linguistics Department at Gallaudet University, for providing her linguistic expertise.

Dr. Clayton Valli, belated and beloved colleague and friend, for providing his encouragement, support, and belief in our book, as well as his poetry.

The faculty and staff members at Gallaudet and Lamar Universities, as well as students and friends, for providing their ongoing support and ideas.

Tamara Davidson, illustrator of this book, for her amazing and creative art work and her years of work on so many, many drafts of this book.

Rosa Lee Gallimore, master signer for our DVD project, for her well-articulated and mesmerizing signed interpretations of Deaf culture.

James DeBee, owner, director, producer and online editor of DeBee Communications Production, for providing his visual motion picture expertise and video production. His production crew Mark Baldivez, Neil Macgill, Don Gaul, and Peter Skarp, for their assistance.

Gary Brooks, owner and producer of Blue Apple Production, for providing visual motion picture expertise and video production for early sections of this project. Jose Saldana for his assistance.

Josh Mendelsohn, for his English to ASL translation of the FBI warning. Jerome Bonheyo, for his clear and concise ASL signing of the FBI warning. Aaron Wegehaupt, for the voice-over of the FBI warning.

Kay Oldfather-Daigle, Kari Bahl, Amy Frasu and Rick Norris for their invaluable voice-over services.

Jacqueline DeBee for her audio mixing, captioning and translating ASL/English services.

Carla Mathers, our lawyer, for tending our legal matters.

Debbie Cruzan, Lisa Frey, Grace (Laird) Shaffer, Donna Scott, and Rachel Graham, personal friends, providing me (Adonia) their loving support.

Summer Crider, Dr. Paul Johnston, Dr. Mike Kemp, Bobby Loeffler, and Audrey Schell, personal friends, for providing me (Lynn) with their loving support.

Barbara 'Bo' Ballard, Josephine Loeffler, Robert and Risa Lewis, and Peter Skarp, our personal friends, for believing in us and promoting our work to the public.

Special thanks to Dr. Kathleen M. Wood, Trudy Suggs and Dr. Vicki Everhart for their careful and professional editing.

The artists, Liz Morris (Not My Choice…Cochlear Implants), the belated Robert L. Johnson (Sugar), Dr. Betty G. Miller (Growth in ASL), and Dr. Paul Johnston (Hand Instrument), for providing use of their paintings for our project.

Chief executive officers, directors and superintendents of schools for the deaf and institutions of higher education: Dr. Ronald Rhoten (Western Pennsylvania School for the Deaf), Russell Fleming (Georgia School for the Deaf), Dr. Angel Ramos (Idaho School for the Deaf), Dr. Elmer Dillingham (Florida School for the Deaf and Blind), Ronald Stern (New Mexico School for the Deaf), James Tucker (Maryland School for the Deaf), Dr. Harvey Corson (American School for the Deaf), Dr. Katherine Jankowski (Laurent Clerc National Deaf Education Center), Sue Hill (Jean Massieu Academy), Dr. Alan Hurwitz (National Technical Institute of the Deaf), Dr. I. King Jordan (Gallaudet University), and Dr. Pam Shaw (Alabama School for the Deaf), for providing use of their institution's names, pictures, and/or logos in our project.

Chairpersons, chief executive officers and presidents of organizations: Leslie Greer (American Sign Language Teachers Association), Jennifer Markel-Woomer (Deaf Bikers of America), Athletic Directors, Coaches, and Sidney Sharp (Mason Dixon Basketball Tournament), Norma Buemi (the national Phi Kappa Zeta sorority), Nancy Bloch and Anita Farb (National Association of the Deaf and Youth Leadership Camp), Barbara Hathaway (Rainbow Alliance of the Deaf), John Maucere (Deafywood) and Dr. Donalda Ammons (Comité International des Sports des Sourds), for providing the use of their organizations' names, pictures, and/or logos in our project.

The president of Gallaudet University, Dr. I. King Jordan, for granting us permission to use his name and poke fun of him in our project.

Ulf Hedberg, Head of the Archives, and Mike Olson, Archives Technician, Gallaudet University Archives, for providing permission to use invaluable cultural information and pictures for our project.

Ruth Reed, an American Sign Language teacher from the Laurent Clerc National Deaf Education Center at Gallaudet University, for assisting and selecting ASL proficient signing children in our project.

Owners of Deaf magazines, Matthew S. Moore (Deaf Life), Benjamin J. Soukup (CSD Spectrum), and Joel Barish (Deaf Nation), and Pamela L. Carmichael (National Technical Institue of the Deaf's Focus), for allowing us to use the covers of their well-known magazines. Joe Dannis for the covers of books produced by the DawnSignPress and Dr. Jean Andrews' children book covers.

Owners of DVDs/Videotapes, Joe Dannis (DawnSignPress) and James DeBee (Los Angels Club for the Deaf).

Persons who provided their pictures and posters, Albert J. Hlibok (Laurent Clerc's Purple Picture), Sherry Hicks and Michael Velez (Half-and-Half Poster).

Dr. Yerker Andersson, Babetta Trapani Popoff, Bonnie Kraft, the late Fred Schreiber and the late George Veditz who gave us an appropriate quote that we are proud to put in our project.

Our belated and beloved heroes' names were included in our project with permissions from Frances Eaton and Barbara Valli (Dr. Clayton Valli), Lauren Lynch-Ryan (Stephen M. Ryan), and Mike Gaido (LeRoy Colombo).

Our dear friends, Grace (Laird) Shaffer, Grant and Misty Laird, and Dr. Eddy Laird, for lending their proud family name for one of the pictures in this project.

Our other dear friends and belated heroes: Charles Thompson, Olof Hanson, Dr. Stephen M. Nover (CAEBER & AEBPD), Dr. Yolanda Rodriquez, Dr. Lawrence Fleischer, Dr. Andrew Foster, George Veditz, Debbie and Garrett Cruzan, Ann Billington Cassell, Sue Livingston, Dr. William C. Stokoe, Laurent Clerc, Thomas H. Gallaudet, people with AIDS, Ernest Hairston, LeRoy Eagle Bear, Joe Dannis, John Carlin, Ann Silver, Uzi Buzgalo, Chuck Baird, Frank Turk, Walter Ripley, Andy Bonheyo, Paul D. Hubbard, Frederick A.P. Barnard, Mabel Hubbard, and Alexander Graham Bell (not our hero but he needs to be mentioned here), whose names appear in our project.

Emily McQuate, Account Executive, who eagerly and patiently waited for us to submit our final project.

Kristen Butler, Project Director, for her undying patience and creative layout.

And importantly, the children and parents assisting this project who dedicated their time by being models of ASL:

Carey and Kassandra Ballard (Rick and Barbara "Bo" Ballard)
Demi Bingham (James and Bonnie Bingham)
Ivana Corey-Genievsky (Alex Genievsky and Rita Corey)

Payne Frankowiak (Joe and Stacia Frankowiak)
Sayre Huddleston (David and Suzanne Huddleston)
Karita Lewis (Robert and Risa Lewis)
Niko Lutes-Stein (Gary Stein and Jeff Lutes)
Alton Jake "AJ" Markel (Jennifer Markel-Woomer)
Emmanuel Perrodin-Njoku (Philip Obi Njoku and Brenda Perrodin)
Hakeem Schiller (James and Donna Schiller)
Freya Seremeth (Bobby Seremeth and Dawn Schriver)
Alexa Simmons (Alex and Jennifer Simmons)
Jamal Whitehurst (Jaron and Julie Whitehurst)

Last, but not least, the hearing kids of Deaf parents (KODAs) assisting this project who also dedicated their time for being voice-overs in our DVD:
Emily DeBee
Jarrod Frank
Patrick Lott

Maurita Obermiller
Darby Talbert

It is not possible to name each and every individual who has helped us with this project, but we deeply appreciate the time each person, school, organization and institution of higher education has contributed.

Although we already mentioned them above, we want to emphasize our expression of deep love and appreciation to our families for their lifetime of caring.

Once again, we thank our parents for teaching us early that we could accomplish even the very difficult things in life. We thank our siblings and their spouses for being wise, gentle, and supportive. We thank our colleagues for their scholarly expertise, intellectual guidance, and loving support. We thank our families and friends for all of their incredible belief and support in this company, ASL Rose.

Introduction

Have You Ever Seen…?: An American Sign Language (ASL) *Handshape DVD/Book* is an American Sign Language (ASL) rhyme DVD/book, similar to English rhyming books such as *The Cat in the Hat* or *Mother Goose Nursery Rhymes*. This whimsical children's book, the first in a series, is designed to be visually pleasing to the deaf reader, just as rhyming phrases are auditorally pleasing to the hearing reader. Illustrations of the ASL rhyming phrases are shown in an animated-sequenced fashion. The illustrations throughout the book also incorporate information about the Deaf community, its culture, and its language.

Have You Ever Seen…? has a companion DVD featuring native ASL users signing the contents of the book. The native signers range in age from three to nine years. Twelve of the signers are Deaf of Deaf parents, and two are hearing children who have Deaf parents (often described as Children of Deaf Adults, or CODAs). Also included on the DVD is information about Deaf culture.

Handshapes

The reports of the number of different handshapes contained within ASL range from approximately 40 to 54 (Battison, 1978; Klima, 1975; Wilbur, 1987). Furthermore, depending upon whether one considers the fine differences in finger movements to constitute different handshapes, the number reported can be as high as 150 distinct handshapes (Liddell & Johnson, 1989). The authors have selected 44 of the most commonly used handshapes, exploring each in this book. Signs can be composed of similar handshapes but differ in meaning due to differences in movement of the handshapes.

There are some handshapes that correspond to English letters, such as E, R, and T. Keep in mind though, that fingerspelling and handshapes are not the same thing. Fingerspelling utilizes specific handshapes to represent English letters. Handshapes are also components of signs in ASL that are completely independent from English. An illustration of each handshape is shown so readers will see how to form each particular handshape (See Figure 1 for an example).

Figure 1. Potato Roller-skating. Handshape Bent V or 2

Deaf Culture

Language and culture cannot be separated. ASL and Deaf Culture co-occur together. ASL is the core of Deaf Culture. Deaf Culture also contains the values, tendencies, folklore, and history of Deaf people. Cultural information about the Deaf community is depicted in each of the illustrations. In addition, details about the cultural information embedded in the illustrations are provided in the column next to each illustration. This is a tool that may be helpful in teaching or sharing Deaf culture with readers.

Signing the Questions/Phrases

Before using this book, it will be practical to know how to translate the phrase "Have you ever seen…?" from English into ASL. The following are

two translations into ASL, which are also demonstrated on the DVD: FINISH SEE YOU? (illustrated in Figure 2) or SEE BEFORE YOU? (illustrated in Figure 3). Either translation is appropriate to use with the phrases in this book.

In ASL, it is crucial to use facial expressions when you ask a question, so be sure to observe the signers' faces closely when watching the DVD. An essential aspect of asking the question, "Have you ever seen…?" is the raising of one's eyebrows. Raised eyebrows always accompany yes/no questions in ASL. This is demonstrated on the DVD and in Figures 2 and 3 below.

Having raised eyebrows requires a head tilt. When you ask a yes-no question, raised eyebrows and a forward head tilt occur at the same time.

For each handshape in "Have You Ever Seen…?", there is a question asked in ASL and in English. For example, the written English text, "Have you ever seen a horse painting?", can be asked in ASL either by signing "HORSE PAINT FINISH SEE YOU?" or "HORSE PAINT SEE BEFORE YOU?"

Be sure to notice how the signer's body must lean forward when asking a question.

Figure 2. FINISH SEE YOU?

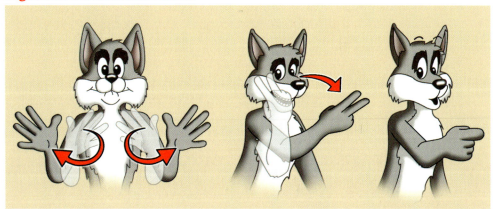

Figure 3. SEE BEFORE YOU?

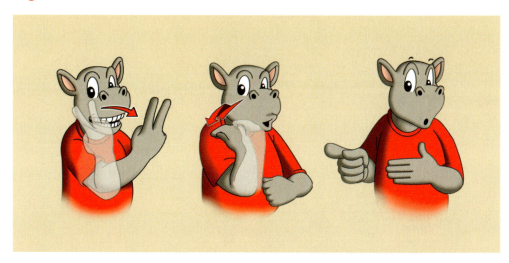

To be grammatically correct in ASL, each phrase in the book is signed before you sign FINISH SEE YOU? (or SEE BEFORE YOU?). Figure 4 illustrates the correct order of the signs in the sentence: HORSE PAINT, FINISH SEE YOU? (or SEE BEFORE YOU?).

Figure 4. Two ASL versions of "Have you ever seen a horse painting?"

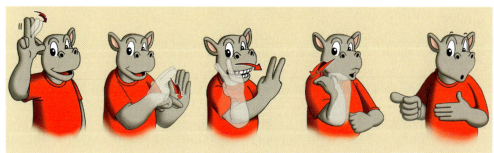

On the DVD and in each page of the book, you will also see a circle showing specific handshape. All the questions illustrated in ASL make use of specific handshapes, and the combination of the ASL signs are translated into English.

A character in each illustration signs an ASL phrase utilizing a specific handshape. Each character's signing is accompanied by facial expression, which, again, is an essential component of ASL. The response, naturally, should be "no" to the silly illustrations and questions. Note that not all illustrations start with the first word of the question. For example, the words "puzzled teeth" are not signed PUZZLED TEETH. Rather, they are signed using a topic-comment format (topic is introduced first with eyebrows raised, then the topic is commented upon or explained with the eyebrows in neutral position): TEETH PUZZLED.

The illustrations in the DVD and the book are relatively the same. However, the DVD also includes several frames related to each handshape. The first frame shows the ASL handshape in isolation. Then, a child will sign the phrase in the picture. The next frame shows another child asking the question, "Have you ever seen?" Finally, you will see the picture from the book and the narrator will explain its significance to Deaf culture. Within each segment, there are culturally rich points and an illustrated character. The character is drawn in light and dark shades to illustrate action or state of the subject. Let's look at an example (Figure 5).

As you can see, there is one character on each page, not two.

Figure 5. Pencil Putting on Lipstick

Sign Movements

Movements involved in producing an ASL phrase are shown in the book by depicting the beginning movement of a phrase in a light-shaded illustration and the ending movement in a dark-shaded illustration. You will also notice red arrows in each illustration. These arrows indicate specific movements made in producing certain signs. The arrows can indicate the following movements of a sign.

1. An arrow can point in the direction that a sign moves.

2. An arrow can show the path that a sign makes.

3. Arrows showing zig-zag movements indicate that a sign movement is repeated at least two times.

4. Curved lines around a sign indicate that the sign is wiggled.

5. Arrows can point in both directions that a sign moves.

Glosses

Since ASL does not yet have a formal written system developed, we have chosen to use glosses—the use of English words in upper-case letters in ASL sign order—to represent ASL in written form. Hyphens between words in a gloss indicate that all the hyphenated words are expressed in a single sign. For example, OPEN-WINDOW is produced as one sign, rather than two separate signs (OPEN, WINDOW). Once again, the DVD may prove to be helpful by demonstrating this in ASL.

Use of Hands

Certain signs may be produced using either one hand or two hands. Try to keep both of your hands free when you are signing. If that is not possible, use the hand which is most comfortable for you. Once you have chosen a dominant hand, be consistent.

Regional Variations

Some of the ASL signs used in your area may differ from those illustrated in the book or shown on the DVD. Just like other languages, ASL has regional variations. For instance, BIRTHDAY has as many as ten variations! Feel free to use the variants of ASL signs common to your region as you read this book.

Let's Get Started!

Ready for a fun adventure? Enjoy viewing the DVD and reading the book!

Description of Front Cover

Each picture on the front cover has a purpose. From right to left, the first picture of a flower teaching represents the authors, who are both teachers. The second illustration is of an elephant, wearing a Gallaudet jersey, cooking. Both of the authors are graduates of Gallaudet University. The third picture shows a horse painting a portrait of Laurent Clerc. Both of the authors admire and respect the achievements of Clerc and his contributions to ASL, and they strive to follow in his footsteps. The fourth picture shows an apple using a TTY. The authors began the development of this DVD/book using TTYs to communicate in English, and then the method of communication progressed to e-mail. Today, the authors communicate regularly via videophone using ASL.

Authors

Adonia K. Smith, Ed.D. candidate and E. Lynn Jacobowitz, Ph.D.

References

Battison, R. (1978). *Lexical borrowing in American Sign Language*. Silver Spring, MD: Linstok Press.

Klima, E. (1975). Sound and its absence in the linguistic symbol. In J.F. Kavanagh & J.E. Cutting (Eds.). *The role of speech in language*. Cambridge, MA: MIT Press.

Liddell, S.K., and Johnson, R.E. (1989). American Sign Language: The phonological base. *Sign Language Studies*, 64, 195-277.

Wilbur, R.B. (1987). *American Sign Language: Linguistic and applied dimensions* (2nd ed.). Boston: College-Hill.

Have you ever seen a donkey opening a window?

The donkey does not feel like going inside to order his food, so he uses the drive-through. Since the drive-through utilizes a speaker and microphone for ordering and is inaccessible to deaf people, the donkey drives past the speaker to order food at the window, where he is given a Braille menu. At fast-food restaurants, workers often give deaf people Braille menus, mistakenly assuming this will help. The donkey writes, "I would like to order..." According to the Americans with Disabilities Act, deaf individuals must be provided reasonable accommodations at all public places.

In the dark-shaded illustration, the donkey signs OPEN-WINDOW so he can communicate by writing back and forth with the wooden door. The signs for DOOR, WOOD, and SPEAKER BOX MACHINE are all produced using the "B" handshape.

Handshape B

Have you ever seen an elephant cooking?

The elephant and the rat are wearing Gallaudet University class jerseys, a tradition at the university. At the start of the year for each freshman class at Gallaudet, class colors and a motto are chosen for use throughout the four years of college for various events. The elephant cooking a rat depicts a good-natured rivalry commonly seen between the student classes. For example, during Homecoming, Spirit Week is held where all the classes compete in various games.

In addition to annual traditions, each student class keeps several secrets that are not to be revealed to any other class. One of the secret traditions used to occur when Gallaudet University had a preparatory program. The preparatory students would hold a mock rat funeral, burying rats (in reality, stuffed animals) to dig up and celebrate at the end of their prepa**RAT**ory year. Another secret tradition involves seniors "kidnapping" class jerseys from other classes in order to bring the jerseys on their senior trip. Their goal is to break the record for the highest number of stolen jerseys. After the trip, the jerseys are returned to their rightful owners, but not before photographs of the jerseys are taken.

These traditions are often some of the fondest memories of Gallaudet alumni.

Handshape
Open B

The blimp is pulling a banner that reads, "ASL *is original like Picasso whereas Signed English is like painting by numbers.*" A well-respected, retired Gallaudet University professor, Dr. Yerker Andersson, is credited with saying this. ASL is a natural and visual-gestural language with its own grammar and visual-spatial principles that are independent from English. ASL is compared to Picasso's art because it is beautiful, natural, and original. "Painting by numbers" figuratively describes Signed English as stilted, unnatural, and artificial. Signed English is one of the Manually Coded English (MCE) systems. Not only is it an artificial communication system, it lacks the grammar of a true, formal language. It is important to note that ASL is *not* English on the hands. The "ASL NOW!" message on the blimp emphasizes that it is time now for ASL to be given full recognition as a legitimate language.

Handshape Bent B

Have you ever seen a pig flying?

Have you ever seen a gorilla acting?

Handshape Open A

One of the most popular Deaf cultural traditions is to participate in skits, storytelling, and drama. Deaf clubs and schools for the Deaf often provide these kinds of entertainment. It is also very important that Deaf entertainment be performed in a "Deaf-friendly" environment, one that enhances visual accessibility. For instance, the Western Pennsylvania School for the Deaf (WPSD) offers high-technology visual access for Deaf people in its theater.

Deafywood, a group of Deaf performers, travels across the United States to perform comedic skits incorporating ASL and Deaf culture. One of *Deafywood's* most popular characters is Superdeafy, played by John Maucere. The gorilla in the picture is wearing an outfit similar to Superdeafy's costume.

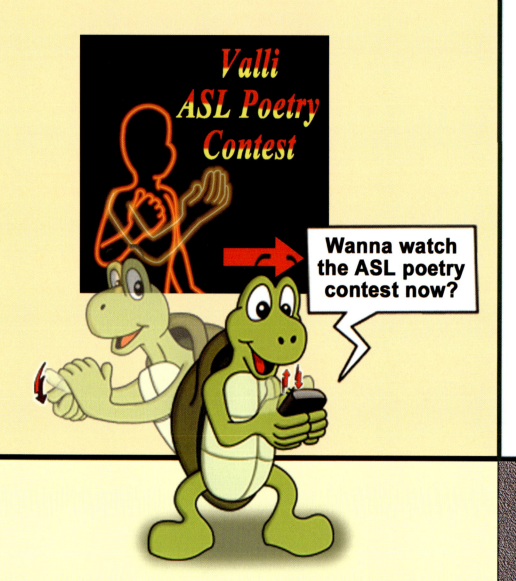

Have you ever seen turtles paging each other?

Handheld wireless pagers equipped with small keyboards are like cellphones for deaf people, providing instant communication using e-mail or text messaging. The turtle's question regarding if the other would like to watch the Valli ASL Poetry Contest at the Deaf club holds cultural significance.

The picture on the wall is of a Deaf club, the Charles Thompson Memorial Hall in St. Paul, Minnesota. Thompson Hall, designed by the late Deaf architect Olof Hanson and built in 1916, is a visually accessible building that is a registered historical landmark in the city of St. Paul. Deaf clubs, during their heyday, were places for Deaf people to gather and enjoy skits, captioned films, card games, and socializing with others who shared their language.

The late Dr. Clayton Valli demonstrated to the world that ASL has its own poetry, with components similar to English's rhymes and line divisions. Components such as use of similar handshapes (rhymes), rhythm of sign movements, and other non-manual signals (facial grammar) are all essential parts of ASL poetry. For more about ASL poetry, the DVD or videotape entitled *ASL Poetry: Selected Works of Clayton Valli* is recommended. The DVD accompanying this book also includes one of Valli's poems, *I'm Sorry*.

Handshape A

The ice cream cone rides past the American Sign Language Teachers Association (ASLTA) building. The sticker on the motorcycle refers to the Deaf Bikers Club, a group of Deaf riders. ASLTA is the only national organization that certifies ASL teachers. One of ASLTA's major goals is to develop an ASL curriculum for Deaf learners. In most deaf schools, English is an integrated part of the curriculum—students learn the rules, grammar, and syntax of English. Without an ASL curriculum, ASL is, as a result, given less emphasis and has a lower status in the educational system compared to English.

Note also the street sign, which refers to the late Stephen M. Ryan (whose name sign is produced with the "S" handshape near the center of the chin), a Deaf comedian fluent in ASL who loved ice cream.

Handshape S

Have you ever seen an ice cream cone riding a motorcycle?

Have you ever seen a toilet getting a tan?

10

The plaque, next to the toilet in this picture, is an actual plaque located in Galveston, Texas, at 54th Street and Seawall Boulevard. It reads, "In memory of LeRoy Colombo." For 40 years, Colombo, the "Hero of Galveston," was a legendary lifeguard who swam like a dolphin, scurried on the sand like a crab, and risked his own life repeatedly to save 907 swimmers from distress. At 12 years of age, LeRoy Colombo made his first rescues when a fire started on a tugboat and spread quickly due to oil around the boat, trapping two men. Colombo, arriving before authorities, braved the burning oil and swam to the men, rescuing them both.

Even though Colombo performed many rescues, he received little recognition during his lifetime. He was given $25 for saving a pet poodle and $30 for recovering a set of dentures from the surf.

Colombo attended the Texas School for the Deaf (TSD) for seven years, where he learned ASL and became part of the Deaf community. In 2002, he was honored posthumously in the Hall of Fame at TSD, and the school swimming pool has been named after him. His achievements are listed in the Guinness Book of World Records and the Texas Book of Records.

Handshape T

On the t-shirt on the floor, there is a button depicting the late Dr. Clayton Valli's famous illustration of "PAH!" "PAH!" in ASL (using the "1" handshape) means "finally" or "it's about time!" This button gained widespread fame when it was used during the 1988 student-led "Deaf President Now" protest at Gallaudet University. During this protest, the students and faculty of Gallaudet University were heard at last and a Deaf president was finally appointed to the only liberal arts university specifically for deaf students in the world.

The "Deaf President Now" (DPN) movement helped to bring about many important laws, such as the 1990 Americans with Disabilities Act (ADA). The ADA provides disabled people equal rights and opportunities. The DPN movement is also believed to have influenced many states pass legislation recognizing ASL as an official language.

Handshape 1

Have you ever seen a mouse brushing her teeth?

Have you ever seen a diamond making a foul?

Handshape D

The Mason-Dixon Basketball Tournament banner hanging on the back wall is commonly displayed at schools for the deaf in the Southeast region. Each deaf school is assigned to certain regions, such as the Central States, Great Plains, and so on. In these regions, states take turns hosting yearly athletic tournaments for deaf schools in their region.

Georgia School for the Deaf (GSD) and Florida School for the Deaf and Blind (FSDB) often compete against each other at the Mason-Dixon tournament, in addition to several other schools in the region.

Deaf people cherish their sporting events, ranging from bowling to basketball to softball. These events are popular gathering opportunities for socialization and fun. They are an integral part of Deaf culture.

13

Have you ever seen birds with fangs?

14

A bird is sitting closely with his family on a telephone line. Deaf families are very often tightly knit. Usually, if a child is born deaf to Deaf parents, the child automatically acquires the unique attributes of Deaf culture. The Deaf culture is a way of life just like other cultures such as Hispanic or Chinese culture. Each culture usually has its own language (or dialect), customs, and way of life that its members live by and value.

A bilingual researcher, Dr. Colin Baker, states succinctly, "A language divorced from its culture is like a body without a soul." Many people mistakenly believe that ASL and Deaf culture isolate deaf children and people from society at large. In reality, the language proficiencies and world knowledge obtained through acquiring ASL and Deaf culture make it easier for a deaf individual to interact with both the Deaf and Hearing worlds. The baby bird holds a sign saying, "Deaf Power," showing that the family is proud to be Deaf and enjoys a special sense of belonging to the Deaf community. There are many Deaf families in the country, such as the Laird family. Deaf families often span many generations, sometimes as many as seven generations!

Handshape G or Q

Have you ever seen a duck wearing a diaper?

The duck is wearing a diaper and a barrette, and these signs are produced using the same "Open N" handshape. Her bib reads, "I am proud to be a CODA," which means she is a child of deaf adults. Babetta Trapani Popoff, a CODA, said, "I am a Deaf person who can hear." Another renowned CODA, Bonnie Kraft, said, "I can hear but my heart is Deaf." CODAs often live in both the Deaf and hearing worlds and benefit from the best in both worlds. Other "ODA" acronyms include KODA (Kid of Deaf Adults), SODA (Sibling or Spouse of Deaf Adults), and GODA (Grandchild of Deaf Adults).

In the toy chest, the stuffed eagle has a t-shirt that reads, "Jean Massieu Academy (JMA)." JMA is a deaf charter school in Arlington, Texas, where both deaf children and CODAs attend school together. The Half-n-Half poster in the background shows dynamic CODAs, Sherry Hicks and Michael Velez, who present original multimedia on aspects of both Deaf and Hearing culture, combining ASL, music, and storytelling.

The wolf is vacuuming up various traditional approaches to teaching Deaf children. These approaches shown are representative of "subtractive" bilingual educational environments because *only* English is taught, the hearing culture is dominant, and the educational policies result in de-valuing ASL and Deaf culture. In contrast, an ASL/English bilingual approach in school represents an "additive" bilingual educational environment where both ASL and English, as well as Deaf and Hearing cultures, are emphasized, taught, and equally valued. This "additive" setting best nurtures and develops Deaf bilinguals. The Center for ASL/English Bilingual Education and Research (CAEBER) at the New Mexico School for the Deaf, under Dr. Stephen M. Nover's guidance, has developed an ASL/English bilingual professional development model for Deaf education. The purpose of the ASL/English bilingual professional development model is to foster leadership in Deaf education and promote Deaf children's acquisition and development of academic proficiency in both ASL and English, as well as the two cultures—Deaf and Hearing. Shown on the bulletin board are essays written by Deaf children about their favorite role models, including Drs. Yolanda Rodriguez, the late Andrew Foster and Larry Fleischer.

On the bulletin board, there is a poster which mentions STAR schools. The USDLC (United Star Distance Learning Consortium) STAR Schools Project is a multi-state project funded by a U.S. Department of Education Star Schools grant. One of its sub-projects was the ASL/English Bilingual Professional Development (AEBPD) program for educators of Deaf students. Schools for the Deaf that have implemented this professional development program are called "Star Schools." These participating schools are Minnesota State Academy for the Deaf; California School for the Deaf, Riverside; Kendall Demonstration Elementary School; and Metro Deaf School, to name a few.

Have you ever seen a wolf vacuuming?

19

Handshape Flattened O

The flower teaches using a bilingual-bicultural approach, learning about ASL, English, and Deaf and Hearing cultures. She is using a bilingual technique called codeswitching: she teaches an English literacy lesson in ASL, then codeswitches to written English using visual technology. She shows that ASL has approximately 44 handshapes and English has 26 letters represented by the manual alphabet. Each language has its own phonology, an aspect of language that deals with the smallest units of contrastive meaning. ASL's cherology (phonology) consists of features such as handshape, palm orientation, movement, location and non-manual signals; while English's phonology is based on sounds. The cherology (phonology) of signed languages is just as complex as that of spoken languages. Visual technologies such as SMART Board, multimedia CD-ROMs, DVDs or DVRs with ASL movies, videoconferencing, and even pagers can be invaluable in the classroom to support literacy instruction and Deaf students' development of both ASL and English.

Have you ever seen a flower teaching?

Have you ever seen an owl knowing nothing?

Handshape O

The owl is wearing a shirt that says ΦΚΖ. ΦΚΖ, or Phi Kappa Zeta, is the oldest Deaf sorority at Gallaudet University, and its mascot is an owl. The sentence "George Veditz wuz here!" is carved on the tree. Veditz was a president of the National Association of the Deaf and is most known for saying, "*As long as we have deaf people on earth, we will have signs...the noblest gift God has given to deaf people.*" Veditz knew ASL was a very special language and helped preserve ASL by being filmed while signing in the early 1900s. Deaf people like Veditz take joy in their language and the Deaf community. They cherish their traditions, beliefs, customs, and values in many ways. Some organizations helping to maintain these traditions, beliefs, customs, and values are Intertribal Deaf Council, National Asian Deaf Congress, National Black Deaf Advocates, Deaf Seniors of America, Deaf Women United, Deaf History International, and American Association of the Deaf-Blind, to name a few.

The carving of "DJ + GC" on the tree refers to Debbie Jarvis and Garrett Cruzan, who are among the many Deaf couples that met at Gallaudet, fell in love, and married.

Handshape
F or 9

As the pineapple, who is Miss Deaf America, walks down the stage, the fox does a double take. The sign for PINEAPPLE shown here may vary according to region.

The Miss Deaf America pageant began in 1972 with only five contestants who were judged on beauty, poise, gracefulness, and cultural talent. Ann Billington was the first Miss Deaf America. After receiving her crown, she devoted her career to teaching ASL. As the number of Miss Deaf America contestants began to grow over the years, the criteria for determining the winner changed. Today, Miss Deaf America contestants are judged based upon private interviews, business attire/platform presentations, talent, and evening gown/on-stage interviews. The pageant is held at the National Association of the Deaf (NAD) convention every two years. During her two-year reign, Miss Deaf America travels throughout the nation and speaks to diverse groups.

Have you ever seen a fox doing a double take?

Have you ever seen a cat interpreting?

As the dog speaks, the cat interprets for the Deaf mouse. The mouse has an umbrella because the dog spits when he talks. The dog is explaining about two pieces of art by Deaf artists. The artwork of the girl crying, drawn by Liz Morris, is entitled *Not My Choice . . . Cochlear Implants*. Liz's art expresses the feelings of a deaf child with hearing parents, who has been implanted without having a choice. The girl's sorrow is due to not being accepted by her hearing parents for who she is before the implant. The sign, "Wrong-Way," describes the isolation and confusion of a child who has been compelled to change her identity in order to conform to society's view of what's best. The artwork on the right wall, *Hand Instrument*, is drawn by Paul Johnston. Johnston draws EYE-music as compared to EAR-music, with the hands as instruments which create visual music. ASL is thus music to Deaf people.

Interpreting (translating from ASL to English or vice versa) for the Deaf community is a popular career choice for hearing people. There are many interpreting preparation programs in the nation as well as interpreting services and agencies. Sue Livingston, a teacher of the Deaf and author of the book, *Rethinking the Education of Deaf Students*, describes how ASL interpreting strategies can be utilized in the classroom to ensure that ideas are clearly expressed and fully comprehensible to Deaf children.

Handshape
Flat F or 9

The deer, standing in front of Chapel Hall at Gallaudet University, is wearing a "Deaf Prez Now" shirt, which refers to the historic 1988 "Deaf President Now" protest at Gallaudet University. The deer, proud of the success of the protest, is applauding visually by waving his hands in the air (the way by which Deaf people applaud). An interesting note is that the four student leaders of the DPN protest shared several commonalities: All were born Deaf to Deaf parents, all attended a residential school for the Deaf, and all were active in extracurricular school activities.

Chapel Hall has the "Tower Clock," in which students often sneak up into to write their names. The building itself is a fine example of polychrome High Victorian Gothic Revival architecture and is a National Historic Landmark. Interestingly, Chapel Hall is where U.S. President James Garfield gave his last public speech a few days before he was killed.

Handshape 5

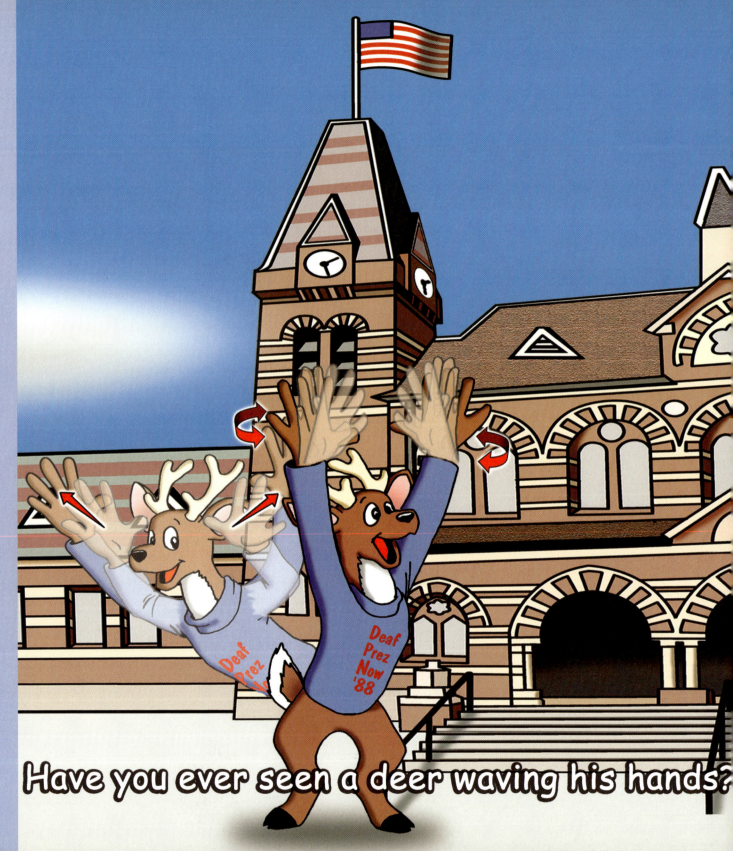

Have you ever seen a deer waving his hands?

26

Have you ever seen a ball's eyes popping out?

The ball shows his shock as he watches *The Three Little Deaf Pigs*, which is closed captioned on television. He has just learned that the wolf has decided to become a friend to one of the three pigs. In this adaptation of the popular story, the wolf is unable to blow down the house made of brick, so he rings the doorbell, which flashes lights inside the house. The Deaf pig opens the door and asks what the wolf wants. The wolf says he is hungry. The Deaf pig cries because he assumes the wolf intends to eat him. The wolf reassures the Deaf pig by explaining that he is hungry to learn ASL, not for food. They become friends, and the wolf is shown on television signing FRIENDS as the pig applauds.

Being able to watch television with closed captioning is a relatively new technological advance in the Deaf community. On the wall behind the ball, there is a National Technical Institute for the Deaf (NTID) calendar, and NTID's *Focus* magazine is on the floor. NTID, part of Rochester Institute of Technology in Rochester, New York, is a technical college for the Deaf.

27

The picture hanging on the wall is a portrait of the late Dr. William C. Stokoe, who is considered the "Father of ASL Linguistics." Stokoe's name sign is formed by placing the "C" handshape on the top of the head and moving it up and down slightly. Stokoe believed that the visual-gestural communication system he witnessed being used by Deaf individuals was a true, complex language. Being the first linguist to study ASL in-depth, his research demonstrated to the world that ASL is a fully developed language with its own grammar. Stokoe's research revealed and described the linguistic structures of ASL, comparable to the structures of all true, formal languages: phonology (cherology), morphology, semantics, syntax, and pragmatics. Unlike English, ASL uses space, facial expressions (non-manual signals), and body movement to express grammar.

Handshape C

Have you ever seen a giraffe with a beard?

And then King Kong signed to Beauty, "Will you marry me? ...Oops!"

The sign for GRASS may vary according to region. The grass laughs when the lion tells a Deaf joke about King Kong. The joke tells of King Kong walking through a city and scaring everyone. When King Kong sees a beautiful woman, he scoops her up in his hands, falling in love with her. The woman points to her ears and shakes her head, indicating that she is deaf. King Kong signs, "Will you marry [one hand coming down to clasp the other] me?" Oops! As he clasps his hands, the woman is flattened in his hands. This is a well-known joke and part of Deaf folklore (or "Deaflore") that has been passed down through generations of the American Deaf community.

Have you ever seen grass laughing?

Have you ever seen a kangaroo who is a pirate?

The kangaroo, traveling on the *Mary Augusta*, is bound for the American School for the Deaf (ASD) in Hartford, Connecticut. ASD, the first Deaf school in America, was founded in 1817 by Laurent Clerc and Thomas H. Gallaudet, who sailed from France to America on the *Mary Augusta*. Clerc later established 41 Deaf schools during his career, and 45 additional schools were founded after his death. The establishment of these schools revolutionized the education of Deaf people in America.

Providing a Deaf Studies curriculum is vital to furnishing Deaf students with valuable historical information about their heritage. Such a curriculum enables Deaf students to learn about Deaf legacies and accomplishments and envision goals for themselves. The late Frederick Schreiber said, *"If Deaf people are to get ahead in our time, they must have a better image of themselves and their capabilities. They need concrete examples of what Deaf people have already done so they can project for themselves a brighter future. If we can have African-American Studies, Jewish Studies, why not Deaf Studies?"*

Handshape Cupped C

Have you ever seen puzzled teeth?

The teeth are confused because they think the brush said "bat." However, the brush really said the word "mat." This is a common error made in lipreading; because many words, such as "bat," "mat," and "pat," look alike on the lips. Lipreading is not a means by which to fully access spoken English.

Sign language is to Deaf people what spoken language is to hearing people. Usually Deaf bilinguals' two languages are a signed language and a written language. Many people hold the misconception that Deaf children need speech to acquire English, which is not supported by research. Spoken language is not necessary for the cognitive and linguistic development of a Deaf child. In 1965, Congress issued the Babbidge Report, which concluded that oral-only Deaf education was a "dismal failure." Many in the Deaf community appreciated this report, and viewed it as a long overdue acknowledgement of the need to incorporate ASL into Deaf education.

The teeth are also shown signing PUZZLED with four fingers. Signers sometimes produce this sign creatively to express extreme confusion or puzzlement, while most signers tend to produce the sign using the index finger only. Other common signs sometimes produced exaggeratedly with four fingers are MUST, STRICT, and SCAR.

Handshape
Bent 4

At the end of the rainbow, the pot holds various colors of eyes and hands. The eyes and hands are valued like gold to Deaf people, because they are essential for visual communication and ASL. The late Fred Schreiber, Executive Director of the National Association of the Deaf and a renowned leader, emphatically stated, *"Ears are not important; it's what's between them that counts."* ASL acquisition for Deaf children is dependent upon visual communication strategies. The earlier a Deaf child is exposed to ASL, the better it is for the child's cognitive and linguistic development. In fact, hearing is not necessary for a Deaf child's language acquisition.

The bird wears a shirt with the Rainbow Alliance of the Deaf (RAD) logo on it. RAD is a national organization for Deaf gay, lesbian, bisexual, and transgender individuals. The quilts shown are representative of the AIDS Memorial Quilt project in Washington, DC, which includes many quilts commemorating Deaf people who have died from AIDS.

Handshape 4

Have you ever seen a rainbow batting her eyelashes?

Deaf Life, CSD *Spectrum*, and *DeafNation* were periodicals about Deaf people's lives and their talents. These periodicals were owned by Deaf entrepreneurs, written by Deaf writers, and edited by Deaf editors; all of whom brought a unique Deaf cultural perspective to the periodicals. On the cover of *Deaf Life* is Ernest Hairston, who has worked at the U.S. Department of Education for more than 25 years. The feature story in the CSD *Spectrum* is about the Sicangu Lakota Sioux Deaf Indian, LeRoy Eagle Bear, who rediscovered his culture, heritage and identity.

Deaf role models are much needed in all professional fields for current and future Deaf generations, and Deaf-run periodicals are a great way of showcasing these role models.

Handshape V or 2

Have you ever seen a pair of scissors reading?

35

Have you ever seen a potato roller-skating?

The potato has a scar on his head where he was implanted with a cochlear implant device. He is wearing a cochlear implant holder that fits around his waist, and he has a noticeable reproduction of the outer transmitter and cords leading to the speech processor.

Many children are increasingly implanted at a young age. Many parents hope that the cochlear implant will help their deaf children "become hearing." Oftentimes, hearing parents want their deaf child to be like other hearing children. They often make statements such as, "If I use ASL, my child will stop using speech," or "The hearing world does not use ASL, so my child must learn to speak and 'listen.'"

Trusted professionals, such as doctors and audiologists, who are usually hearing themselves, have few or no Deaf adult friends, and know little about ASL or Deaf culture. Due to their own biases, many doctors believe that deaf people need to be fixed so they will "fit in" with hearing society. The belief that speech is superior to ASL is called "audism" and is analogous to racism and sexism. "Hearization" is the term that describes the process whereby deaf children are forced to imitate the unnatural language behaviors, and conform to the preferences, expectations, values, perspectives, and characteristics of the auditory-based, hearing world.

The sign for COCHLEAR IMPLANT uses the "Bent V or 2" handshape. Utilizing the same handshape is the sign for SNAKE, GUM and DOLLAR-EYES. The snake in the background of the illustration has dollar signs for its eyes, representing some in the medical profession who often are not familiar educated about Deaf culture and view the cochlear implant as a means of financial gain.

Handshape
Bent V or 2

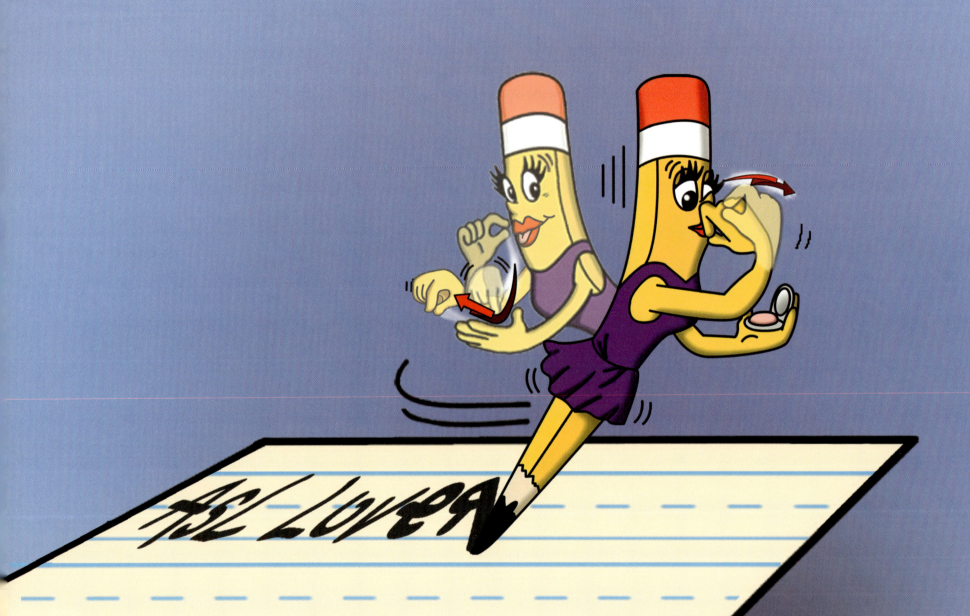

Have you ever seen a pencil putting on lipstick?

The pencil writes as if she is an elementary-aged writer who reverses her R's. At the same time, the pencil shows that she is proud of being an ASL user by writing "ASL Lover" in English, her second language. With the development of both languages nurtured, respected, and supported, she can easily become a balanced bilingual—competent in both ASL and written English. ASL does not yet have a formal written form, so she enjoys writing and reading in English. Dr. Jim Cummins, a well-known bilingual researcher, has found considerable support for his theory that skills in one language can transfer to a second language. ASL can serve as a deaf child's first language, with English introduced as a second language. In cases where English is the deaf child's first language, ASL can be introduced as a second language. Deaf bilinguals value the significance of both ASL and written English. The key to successful bilingual education is both languages being respected and nurtured *equally*. Deaf children often grow up to be successful Deaf adults if they have access to quality bilingual education that uses both ASL and English as languages of instruction.

Handshape Modified X

The apple calls his friend using a teletypewriter device for the Deaf (TDD or TTY) that connects to the onion's computer. There are many hidden "X" handshapes in this illustration. The worm coming out of the apple is signed using the "X" handshape. The sign for TEXAS and PHOENIX both use the "X" handshape. The sign for ONION and TEARDROP is also signed using the "X" handshape.

Deaf individuals presently use TTYs, computers, and web- or television-based cameras to communicate with each other. Once a staple in practically every deaf household, now TTYs are decreasing in use due to the advent of computers, instant messaging (IM), and visual communication devices like the videophone.

Handshape X

Have you ever seen an apple calling an onion?

The egg, wearing a necktie displaying the "I-LOVE-YOU" symbol, is selling books, videotapes and DVDs that relate to ASL, Deaf history, Deaf culture, and the Deaf community. DawnSignPress, run by owner Joe Dannis, is an example of a successful Deaf-owned business. Other successful Deaf-owned businesses include Harris Communications, DeBee Communications, T.S. Writing Services and Anita Kroll Interiors. Due to the growth of Deaf-owned businesses, the National Deaf Business Institute was founded to provide a directory of Deaf-owned businesses, a mentorship program, and workshops.

Have you ever seen an egg wearing a necktie?

Have you ever seen a horse painting?

The horse is painting a portrait of Laurent Clerc, the Deaf teacher who helped to establish the first school specifically for Deaf students in America. Clerc's sign name is formed using the "Closed 3" handshape by brushing the fingers down twice on the cheek, with the thumb sticking out, imitating the facial scar he had. The charcoal drawing of Clerc on the wall was drawn by the late Deaf artist John Carlin. Carlin Hall, one of its six dormitories, is named by Gallaudet University in commemoration of John Carlin.

A Deaf Visual Arts Image (De'VIA) Classroom poster is on the bulletin board. De'VIA, or Deaf art, is a design that Deaf artists sometimes apply to their work to symbolize their experiences of being a Deaf individual and their pride in being part of the Deaf community. De'VIA art mediums vary from painting to pottery to photography to sculpting. Deaf artists, such as Ann Silver, Uzi Buzgalo, Susan Dupor, and Chuck Baird, are listed on the poster as special guests.

Handshape Closed 3

The rooster is in a rocking chair next to a treasure chest that has "Martha's Vineyard" written on it. The chest holds a wealth of information about Martha's Vineyard, an island located off the Massachusetts coast. A large Deaf community once lived on Martha's Vineyard, and island residents developed a sign language, Martha's Vineyard Sign Language (MVSL). Because of the prevalence of deaf people, MVSL was used by everyone on the island regardless of whether they were Deaf or hearing. Eventually, a combination of MVSL, French Sign Language (brought to America by Laurent Clerc), and mainland signs evolved into what is known today as ASL.

On the wall, a piece of art by Deaf artist Betty Miller, entitled *Growth in* ASL, shows the sign GROW, expressing the idea that ASL is growing stronger every day.

Handshape 3

Have you ever seen a rooster in a rocking chair?

Handshape Bent 3

The bug, wearing a cycling uniform, is standing on a podium that shows the word "Deaflympics". The founding organization, Comité International des Sports des Sourds (CISS), oversees the international Deaflympics (formerly known as World Games for the Deaf, then Deaf World Games). CISS is the oldest existing sports organization for disabled people recognized by the International Olympic Committee (IOC).

Deaflympics, founded in Paris in 1924 and held every four years, is equivalent to the Olympics for deaf people. The summer and winter Deaflympics offer a number of sports: track and field, basketball, cycling, handball, swimming, and other sports for summer; skiing, snowboarding, ice hockey, and some other sports for winter.

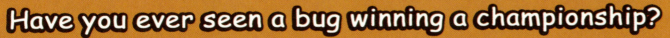

Have you ever seen a bug winning a championship?

45

Handshape Bent L

    The moon is working as a relay operator so the Deaf and hearing stars can communicate with each other via phone and computer. The Deaf star communicates with a relay operator via computer and video camera. The moon relay operator speaks everything the Deaf star signs to the hearing star and signs everything the hearing star speaks to the Deaf star.

    Relay services, provided by the Americans with Disabilities Act, have allowed Deaf people to have nearly equal, 24-hour, access to communication by phone. The types of relay services available today are landline telephone/TTY, Internet, and videophone. We can only imagine what will be next!

Have you ever seen a moon working as a relay operator?

Have you ever seen a hair dryer welding?

The hair dryer is welding the National Association of the Deaf (NAD) logo. At the 1880 World Congress for the Deaf in Milan, Italy, more than 150 hearing delegates lobbied against the use of signed languages in Deaf education classrooms because they mistakenly believed that signed languages were inferior. They successfully voted to approve a resolution forbidding the use of signed languages in Deaf education and advocating the oral method (using speech only). The conference was secretly planned so Deaf people would not participate. Since Deaf people were mostly unaware of the Conference, only one Deaf representative attended.

As a consequence of the sweeping changes in Deaf education, many Deaf people and hearing signers lost their teaching positions or were demoted in their jobs. Deaf people's English literacy levels also may have deteriorated because of the ban on signed languages in educational settings. Many Deaf people viewed the Milan conference resolution as a travesty of justice. This led to the establishment of the National Association of the Deaf (NAD) in 1880, the oldest and largest constituency organization safeguarding accessibility and civil rights of 28 million Deaf and hard-of-hearing Americans in the areas of advocacy, education, employment, health care, and telecommunications.

Handshape
I-L or I-L-Y

The airplanes, flying over Gallaudet University, are expressing their love for each other by using the universal sign for "I Love You." However, sign language is not universal. Different countries have different signed languages, just like spoken languages differ from country to country. However, signed languages throughout the world share similar linguistic features such as use of handshapes, location, non-manual signals, movement, and space.

Seen below the airplanes are Gallaudet's landmark Tower Clock, the U.S. Capitol, and the Washington Monument. Gallaudet University is the world's only liberal arts university specifically for Deaf people and is located in the nation's capital, Washington, DC.

Have you ever seen two airplanes falling in love?

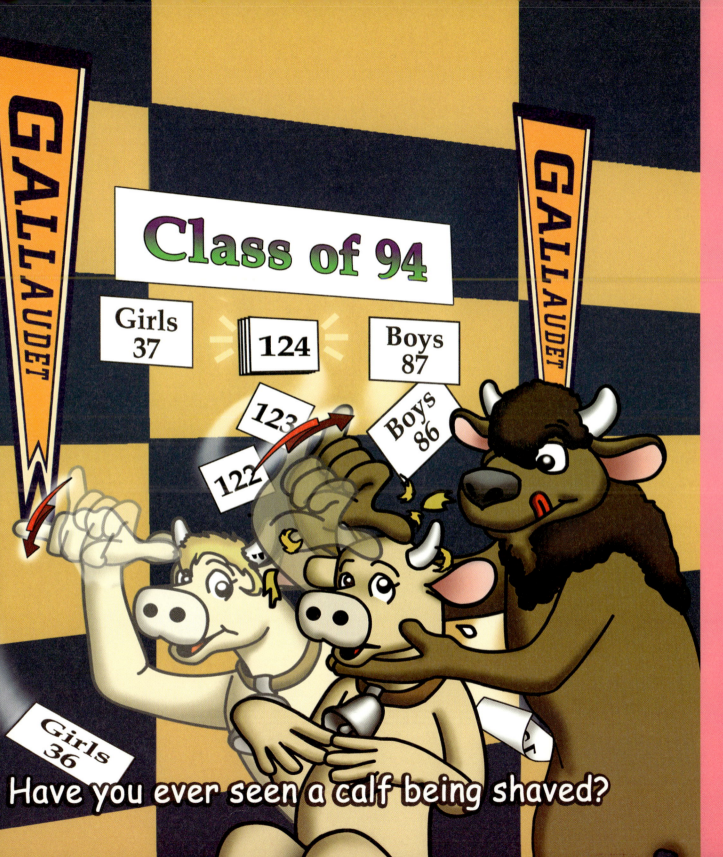

Class of 94

Girls 37 |124| Boys 87

123   122   Boys 86

Girls 36

Have you ever seen a calf being shaved?

Handshape Y

The bison is the mascot of Gallaudet University. A tradition at Gallaudet University is to have freshmen voluntarily shave their heads at the end of their first year and become "true Gallaudetians." On "Bald Day," each freshman class strives to break the record of most shaved heads, for both males and females. The BISON sign is formed in the "Y" handshape on the forehead, and the SHAVE (as in shaving head) sign is formed by the "Y" handshape going backwards over the head.

Have you ever seen a hippo mocking kids?

Handshape
I-1

Deaf campers sit in a circle around a bonfire during a Junior National Association of the Deaf (Jr. NAD) Youth Leadership Camp (YLC). YLC, founded by "Father of Deaf Youth Leadership" Dr. Frank Turk, is a popular camp for young leaders to come together and learn leadership skills along with team-building strategies. Originally held in Pennsylvania, the camp has been held in several different locations, including Minnesota, Oregon, South Dakota and Florida.

The campers share A-Z stories about ghosts while the hippo plays tricks on them. The sign for HIPPO may vary from region to region, using either the "I-1" handshape or the "Y" handshape. A-Z stories, popular in Deaf culture, are told using the handshapes of each letter of the manual alphabet, starting with A and ending with Z. See Jacobowitz's excerpt, A-Z story, *Baby and Mother*, on the DVD.

Have you ever seen a rhino walking in high heels to a Deaf school?

Handshape I

The rhino, standing by the Idaho School for the Deaf and the Blind sign in Gooding, is signing RHINO. She also shows that she is walking in high heels by using the "I" handshape to indicate the heels. Rhinos are typically heavy, but the female rhino here is thin. THIN is also signed by using the "I" handshape.

The same handshape is used to sign INSTITUTE which refers to schools for the Deaf, or "Deaf schools." Deaf schools carry rich history and resources of Deaf culture. In regards to preserving Deaf culture, no other type of school or program can compare to Deaf schools.

Handshape Modified 8

The heart is attempting to talk to his friend via the Internet as his friend is trying to put on contact lenses. Eye contact is very important when communicating in ASL. The heart signs HEART (shown in light shade), and WHAT-UP? (shown in dark shade). The signs for TECHNOLOGY, INTERNET, CONTACT LENSES, and EYE CONTACT are produced using the "Modified 8" handshape.

On the floor is a sign saying, "Welcome to the Union League Deaf Club." Deaf clubs, which were gathering spots at specific locations for Deaf people, were very popular from the 1900s until the late 1980s. The spider webs around the sign show how Deaf clubs have lost their popularity, mostly due to advances in communication technology. The Union League (UL) in New York City was the oldest club for the Deaf in the United States. Next to the computer is a videotape of a documentary about the Los Angeles Club for the Deaf, another legendary Deaf club.

The picture of Sugar signing I-LOVE-YOU was drawn by a talented artist, the late Robert L. Johnson (his name sign was R-J, fingerspelled). Robert modeled the Sugar character after his wife, Liz Morris, who is also a successful artist.

Have you ever seen a heart asking, "What's up?"

Handshape 8

The meat is telling a story using *Have You Ever Seen...? An American Sign Language* (ASL) *Handshape* DVD/*Book* during "storytelling hour" at a local bookstore. Today, it is common to have these storytelling hours at bookstores where Deaf, ASL storytellers sign stories incorporating Deaf culture for the local Deaf, as well as hearing, communities.

Storytelling is the most popular form of signed entertainment in the body of ASL literature that includes stories, poems, folklore, riddles, humor, and other genres, in ASL only, that have been passed on from one generation to another by Deaf people. Storytelling includes handshape stories, A-Z or number stories, one-handshape stories, narratives, and many other types. See Jacobowitz's number story, *Thirsty*, on the DVD. There are also ASL/English bilingual DVDs and books (presented in both ASL and English), such as *Deaf Cinderella* and *Deaf Coach Now*.

Have you ever seen meat telling a story?

59

Handshape
Open 8

The bees on the sideline are huddling under a towel so the other deaf school's players cannot see them signing. A historic game took place in 2000 between the Alabama School for the Deaf (ASD) and the Maryland School for the Deaf-Frederick (MSD-F)—both with exceptional football teams. The coaches of both schools, Walter Ripley (ASD) and Andy Bonheyo (MSD-F), happened to be brothers-in-law.

It is believed that Paul D. Hubbard, a football player at Gallaudet University, invented the huddle during the 1890s. Soon after Paul's invention, other teams began using the huddle, which is still used to this day. A drum is often used during football games to let the players know when to snap the ball.

Football games between deaf schools are often great attractions, bringing in full crowds cheering for their favorite teams.

Have you ever seen a bee kicking a football?

I. King Jordan is the first Deaf president of Gallaudet University. His sign name, and the sign KING, are formed using the "K or P" handshape.

Frederick A.P. Barnard was the first Deaf president of a university in the United States. He presided over the Columbia College (now Columbia Teachers University) during the 1800s. LAMB, SKUNK, and BABYSIT are signed using the "K or P" handshape.

**Handshape
K or P**

Have you ever seen a skunk babysitting King?

EYEth

EARth

Have you ever seen a rocket wearing braids?

The rocket is leaving the oppression she faced on the hearing-focused EARth and is on her way to the planet EYEth. EYEth is a popular fictitious planet among the Deaf community. EYEth's population consists mostly of Deaf people, who use their eyes and hands to communicate. Through language, culture and traditions, Deaf people come together to form the community. The official language of education, politics, and media is ASL which is also the domestic language; while English is taught as a foreign language. On EYEth, the established laws reflect Deaf cultural norms, and visual access to information and events is maximized.

When children are born hearing on EYEth, ASL therapists and specialists are immediately brought in. These children are tested in order to diagnose their tragic hearing disability—which has no cure. However, Deaf scientists and doctors have been working on a new medical technology—the ulna channel 44 implant, which is placed on hearing children if they cannot sign fluently. Parents everywhere are relieved with the seeming success of this implant. Otherwise, their hearing children will have to be sent to EARth with all other hearing people, isolated from the Deaf world.

Although the above is written humorously, it is an analogy to the experiences that some Deaf people have recounted for decades.

Handshape R

The $6 bill has a portrait of Alexander Graham Bell. He believed that Deaf people should be forbidden from marrying each other in order to prevent the reproduction of deaf children. Ironically, he was a CODA—his mother was Deaf—and he married an oral Deaf woman, Mabel. He was also a fluent signer. The telephone was invented by accident when Bell tried to invent a device to enable his wife to hear. Using his fame as influence, he attempted to end ASL/English bilingual education. For the rest of his life, Bell proclaimed that the (English-only) oral method was a proper system for educating Deaf children. This "subtractive" (English-only) oral method resulted in the deterioration of thousands of Deaf children's education over the years.

Handshape W or 6

Have you ever seen a pea-brained $6 bill?

Have you ever seen an
En-DEAF-Quirer creating EEE sounds?

Handshape E

The *En-DEAF-Quirer* magazine wears a hearing aid, unaware that the hearing aid is making a piercing ringing sound. The headline on the front cover of the magazine is "CI [Cochlear Implants] Can Make You Hear 110%!"—an unrealistic expectation. In fact, the Food and Drug Administration (FDA) has released a warning that cochlear implants can sometimes result in bacterial meningitis, which may result in death. Other exaggerated or false stories in the tabloid include "Signed English is 100% Comprehensible," "Oral Method Makes Your Deaf Child Look Hearing" and "SIM-COM [speaking and signing at the same time] Is a Natural and Comprehensible Language!" These stories poke fun at some of the claims of professionals advocating (English-only) oral methods that lack substantial research support. For example, there is no good evidence that learning sign language harms development of speech skills. In fact, several studies have found a positive correlation between deaf students' ASL proficiency and English competency.

References

Handshape B (page 1)

. . . a donkey opening a window?

- National Association of the Deaf. (2000). *Legal rights: The guide for deaf and hard of hearing people* (5th ed.). Washington, DC: Gallaudet University Press.
- *Title III of the ADA: Provision of auxiliary aids.* (n.d.). Retrieved April 20, 2004, from http://www.nad.org/infocenter/infotogo/legal/ada3aux.html.

Handshape Open B (page 2)

. . . an elephant cooking?

- Holmes, T. (2002, August 22). Traditions at Gallaudet. *The Buff and Blue*, pp. 32–33.
- Todd, C., & Valdez, G. (1987, Spring). Rat funeral party a success. *Knob Hill News*, pp. 1–2.

Handshape Bent B (page 4)

. . . a pig flying?

- Supalla, S. (1991). Manually Coded English: The modality question in signed language development. In P. Siple & S. Fisher (Eds.), *Theoretical issues in sign language research, Volume 2: Psychology* (pp. 85–109). Chicago: University of Chicago Press.

Handshape Open A (page 5)

. . . a gorilla acting?

- Brubaker, D. (1999, September/October). Rated D: Kentucky students roar at Deafywood III. *World Around You*, p. 14.
- Padden, C., & Humphries, T. (1988). *Deaf in America: Voices from a culture.* Cambridge, MA: Harvard University Press.

- Peters, C. (2000). *Deaf American literature: From carnival to the canon.* Washington, DC: Gallaudet University Press.
- Schuchman, J. (1988). *Hollywood speaks: Deafness and the film entertainment industry.* Urbana, IL: University of Illinois Press.

Handshape A (page 6)

. . . turtles paging each other?

- Busenbark, J. (Spring 2002). Deaf Minnesotans reflect on 85 years at Thompson Hall. CSD *Spectrum*, 2(1), p. 10.
- Fortt, J. (2003, May 8). SideKick, other devices benefit the deaf. *The Mercury News.* Retrieved May 8, 2003, from http://www.mercurynews.com.
- Valli, C. (1996). ASL *poetry: Selected works of Clayton Valli* [Videotape]. San Diego, CA: DawnSignPress.
- Valli, C. (1996). Poetics of ASL poetry. In V. Walters (Ed.), *Deaf studies IV: Visions of the past—Visions for the future* (pp. 253–263). Washington, DC: Gallaudet University College for Continuing Education.

Handshape S (page 8)

. . . an ice cream cone riding a motorcycle?

- Jacobowitz, E.L. (2005). American Sign Language Teacher Education Preparation Programs. *Sign Language Studies*, 6(1), 76–110.
- Drasgow, E. (1998). American Sign Language as a pathway to linguistic competence. *Exceptional Children*, 64(3), 329–342.
- McKenna, D. (1995, June 9). Deaf comedy jam: Stephen Ryan's humor falls on deaf ears. *Washington City Paper*, p. 9.
- Pendlebury, W. (2003, October). Deaf bikers riding in America. SIGNews, p. 8.
- Wallinger, L. (2000). American Sign Language instruction: Moving from protest to practice. *NECTFL Review*, 48, 27–36.

Handshape T (page 10)
. . . a toilet getting a tan?
- Allen, G.B. (1926, June). The silent worker. *Athletics*, 38(9), 418–420.
- Carroll, C., & Mather, S.M. (1997). *Movers & shakers: Deaf people who changed the world*. San Diego, CA: DawnSignPress.

Handshape 1 (page 12)
. . . a mouse brushing her teeth?
- Gannon, J.R. (1989). *The week the world heard Gallaudet*. Washington, DC: Gallaudet University Press.
- Ramos, A. (2003). *Triumph of the spirit: The DPN chronicle*. Twin Falls, ID: R & R.

Handshape D (page 13)
. . . a diamond making a foul?
- Gannon, J.R. (1981). *Deaf heritage: A narrative history of deaf America*. Silver Spring, MD: National Association of the Deaf.
- Stewart, D. (1991). *Deaf sports: The impact of sports within the deaf community*. Washington, DC: Gallaudet University Press.

Handshape G or Q (page 14)
. . . birds with fangs?
- Baker, C. (2001). *Foundations of bilingual education and bilingualism* (3rd ed.). Clevedon, England: Multilingual Matters.
- Bangs, D. (1995). *A deaf family diary*. Washington, DC: SignRise Cultural Arts.
- Carpenter, D. (1994, April 13). Signer of the declaration. *The Indianapolis Star*, pp. A1, A6.
- Schneider, J. (2000, Spring). The best of all worlds. *Careers & the Disabled*, 14(3), 24–26.

Handshape Open N (page 16)
. . . a duck wearing a diaper?
- Bull, T. (1998). *On the edge of deaf culture: Hearing children/deaf parents*. Alexandria, VA: Deaf Family Research Press.
- Carter, O. (2002, October 10). *Charter school for deaf is proud of its successes*. Retrieved March 4, 2004, from http://www.dfw.com/mld/startelegram/news/columists/ok_carter/4252298.htm.
- Kraft, B. (1997). *Tomorrow dad will still be deaf and other stories* [Videotape]. San Diego, CA: DawnSignPress.

Handshape Open O (page 18)
. . . a wolf vacuuming?
- Bailes, C.N. (2001). Integrative ASL-English language arts: Bridging paths to literacy. *Sign Language Studies*, 1(2), 147–174.
- Nover, S.M., Andrews, J.F., Baker, S., Everhart, V.S., & Bradford, M. (2002). *Staff development in ASL/English bilingual instruction for deaf students: Evaluation and impact study*. USDLC Star Schools Project Report No. 5. Retrieved April 4, 2005, from http://www.nmsd.k12.nm.us/caeber/documents/year5.pdf.
- Stokoe, W. (1989). Dimensions of differences: ASL and English-based cultures. In S. Wilcox (Ed.), *American deaf culture*. Silver Spring, MD: Linstok Press.

Handshape Flattened O (page 20)
. . . a flower teaching?
- Brisk, M.E., & Harrington, M.M. (2000). *Literacy and bilingualism: A handbook for all teachers*. Mahwah, NJ: Lawrence Erlbaum.
- Crystal, D. (2003). *A dictionary of linguistics & phonetics*. Blackwell, England: Oxford University.
- Fountas, I.C. & Pinnell, G.S. (1996). *Guided reading: Good first teaching for all children*. Portsmouth, NH: Heinemann.

- Gallimore, L. (1999). *Teachers' stories: Teaching American Sign Language and English literacy*. Unpublished doctoral dissertation, University of Arizona, Tucson.
- Padden, C. (1998). Early bilingual lives of deaf children. In I. Parasnis (Ed.), *Culture and language diversity and the deaf experience* (pp. 99–116). New York: Cambridge University Press.

Handshape O (page 21)

. . . an owl knowing nothing?

- Ness, V. (1997). *The preservation of American Sign Language* [Videotape]. Burtonsville, MD: Sign Media.
- Scott, D. (1961, Fall). The Phi Kappa Zeta sorority: Its past and present. *Gallaudet Alumni Bulletin*, 7(1), 8–10.

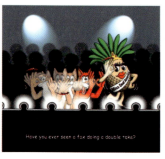

Handshape F or 9 (page 22)

. . . a fox doing a double take?

- Broadwell, B. (2002, March 14). Ann Billington-Bahl: Miss Deaf America 30 years later. Retrieved June 4, 2004, from http://www.icanonline.net.
- Gannon, J.R. (1981). *Deaf heritage: A narrative history of deaf America*. Silver Spring, MD: National Association of the Deaf.
- Lucas, C. (1997). Linguistic variation in ASL: An overview. In C. Carroll (Ed.), *Deaf studies V: Toward 2000—unity and diversity* (pp. 163–185). Washington, DC: Gallaudet University College for Continuing Education.

Handshape Flat F or 9 (page 24)

. . . a cat interpreting?

- Bienvenu, M.J. (1987). The third culture: Working together. *Journal of Interpretation*, 4, 1–12.
- Lane, H., Hoffmeister, R., & Bahan, B. (1996). *A journey into the DEAF-WORLD*. San Diego, CA: DawnSignPress.
- Livingston, S. (1997). *Rethinking the education of deaf students: Theory and practice from a teacher's perspective*. Portsmouth, NH: Heinemann.

- Schertz, B., & Lane, H. (2000). Elements of a culture: Visions by deaf artists. *Journal of the Society for Visual Anthropology: Visual Anthropology Review*, 15(2), 20–36.

Handshape 5 (page 26)

. . . a deer waving his hands?

- My adventure in the tower clock. (1967, October 27). *Buff and Blue*, p. 3.
- Did you know? It's presidential. (2000, Spring). *Gallaudet Today*, 30(2), 34–35.
- Gannon, J.R. (1989). *The week the world heard Gallaudet*. Washington, DC: Gallaudet University Press.
- Maddex, D. (1973). *Historic buildings of Washington, D.C.* Pittsburgh, PA: Ober Park Associates.

Handshape Bent 5 or Claw (page 27)

. . . a ball's eyes popping out?

- Jacobowitz, E.L. (in press). *The three little deaf pigs* [DVD & Book]. Frederick, MD: ASL Rose.
- Lang, H., & Conner, K. (2001). *From dream to reality: The National Technical Institute for the Deaf, a college of Rochester Institute of Technology*. Rochester, NY: Rochester Institute of Technology.
- McCann, J. (2002, June/July). From captioned films to captioned TV. . . *NADmag*, 2(2), 16–17.
- Wiesner, D. (2001). *The Three Pigs*. New York: Clarion Books.

Handshape C (page 28)

. . . a giraffe with a beard?

- Maher, J. (1996). *Seeing language in sign: The work of William C. Stokoe*. Washington, DC: Gallaudet University Press.
- Stokoe, W. (1960). *Sign language structure: An outline of visual communication systems of the American deaf*. Burtonsville, MD: Linstok Press.

- Valli, C., & Lucas, C. (2000). *Linguistics of American Sign Language*: An introduction (3rd ed.). Washington, DC: Gallaudet University Press.

Handshape Open C (page 29)

. . . grass laughing?

- Holcomb, R., Holcomb, S., & Holcomb, T. (1994). *Deaf culture, our way*: *Anecdotes from the deaf community* (3rd ed.). San Diego, CA: DawnSignPress.
- Jacobowitz, E.L. (1992). Humor and wit in the deaf community. In J. Cebe (Ed.), *Deaf studies*: *What's up?* (pp. 187–192). Washington, DC: Gallaudet University College for Continuing Education.
- Jacobowitz, E.L. & Smith, A.K. (in press). *Deaf King Kong* [DVD & Book]. Frederick, MD: ASL Rose.
- Shroyer, E., & Shroyer, S. (1984). *A look at regional differences in American Sign Language*: *Signs across America*. Washington, DC: Gallaudet College Press.

Handshape Cupped C (page 30)

. . . a kangaroo who is a pirate?

- Bienvenu, M.J. (1993). Deaf studies in the Year 2000: New directions. In J. Cebe (Ed.), *Deaf studies* III: *Bridging cultures in the 21st century* (pp. 7–18). Washington, DC: Gallaudet University College for Continuing Education.
- DeBee, J.R. (1995). *Schools for the deaf* [Videotape]. Pittsburgh, PA: DeBee Communications.
- Katz, C. (2002). *A history of the establishment of three Bachelor of Arts degree-granting deaf studies programs in America*. Unpublished doctoral dissertation, Lamar University, Beaumont, TX.
- Schein, J. (1981). *A rose for tomorrow*: *Biography of Frederick C. Schreiber*. Silver Spring, MD: National Association of the Deaf.
- Young, B. (1997). *The chain of love*. Bloomfield, CT: P&S Services.

Handshape Bent 4 (page 32)

. . . puzzled teeth?

- Andersson, R. (1994). Second language literacy in deaf students. In I. Ahlgren & K. Hyltenstam (Eds.), *Bilingualism in deaf education* (pp. 91–101). Hamburg, Germany: Signum.

- Babbidge, H.D. (1965). *Education of the deaf in the United States*: A *report to the secretary of health, education and welfare by his advisory committee of education of the deaf*. Washington, DC: U.S. Government Printing Office.
- Ladd, P. (2003). *Understanding deaf culture*: *In search of deafhood*. Clevedon, England: Multilingual Matters.

Handshape 4 (page 34)

. . . a rainbow batting her eyelashes?

- Lane, H., Hoffmeister, R., & Bahan, B. (1996). *A journey into the DEAF-WORLD*. San Diego, CA: DawnSignPress.
- Luczak, R. (Ed.). (1993). *Eyes of desire*: A *deaf gay & lesbian reader*. Los Angeles: Alyson Publications.
- Mundy, L. (2002, March 31). A world of their own. *The Washington Post Magazine*, p. 22–29 & 38–43.
- Schein, J. (1981). *A rose for tomorrow*: *Biography of Frederick C. Schreiber*. Silver Spring, MD: National Association of the Deaf.

Handshape V or 2 (page 35)

. . . a pair of scissors reading?

- Moore, M., & Levitan, L. (1996, August). Ernie Hairston celebrates 25 years with the U.S. Department of Education. *Deaf Life*, 9(2), 10–23.
- Moore, M., & Panara R. (1996). *Great deaf Americans* (2nd ed.). New York: Deaf Life Press.
- Paris, D. (1999, June). Efforts underway for Laurent Clerc stamp. *DeafNation*, pp. 1, 8.
- Bear, L.E. (Fall/Winter 2004). Reclaiming my true heritage. *CSD Spectrum*, pp. 12–13.

Handshape Bent V or 2 (page 36)

. . . a potato roller-skating?

- Lane, H. (1992). Cochlear implants are wrong for young deaf children. In M. Garreston (Ed.), *Viewpoints on deafness—A deaf American monograph* (pp. 89–92). Silver Spring, MD: National Association of the Deaf.

- Lane, H., Hoffmeister, R., & Bahan, B. (1996). The hearing agenda II: Eradicating the DEAF-WORLD. In L. Bragg (Ed.), *Deaf world: A historical reader and primary sourcebook* (pp. 365–379). New York: New York University Press.
- Nover, S.M. (1995). Politics and language: American Sign Language and English in deaf education. In C. Lucas (Ed.), *Sociolinguistics in deaf communities* (pp. 109–163). Washington, DC: Gallaudet University Press.

Handshape Modified X (page 38)

. . . a pencil putting on lipstick?

- Andrews, J.F., Leigh, I.W., & Weiner, M.T. (2004). *Deaf people: Evolving perspectives from psychology, education and sociology.* Boston: Allyn and Bacon.
- Bailes, C. (1999). Deaf-centric teaching: A case study in ASL/English bilingualism. In L. Bragg (Ed.), *Deaf world: A historical reader and primary resource book* (pp. 211–233). New York: New York University Press.
- Nover, S.M., Christensen, K.M., & Cheng, L.L. (1998). Development of ASL and English competence for learners who are deaf. In K. Bulter & P. Prinz (Eds.), ASL proficiency and English language acquisition: New perspectives [Special issue]. *Topics in Language Disorders*, 18(4), 61–72.

Handshape X (page 40)

. . . an apple calling an onion?

- Cagle, S., & Cagle, K. (1991). *GA and SK etiquette: Guidelines for telecommunications in the deaf community.* Bowling Green, OH: Bowling Green Press.
- Paul, F.A., & Bahan, B.J. (1990). *The American Sign Language handshape game cards.* San Diego, CA: DawnSignPress.

Handshape U or H (page 41)

. . . an egg wearing a necktie?

- Franklin, M. (2001, September). House dreams dare to come true at AKI interiors. *Silent News*, pp. 12, 15.
- Suggs, T. (2001, December). From sports to psychology to sales. *Silent News*, pp. 1, 27.

- Suggs, T. (2003, Fall). The man behind DawnSignPress. *Deaf Success Magazine*, 1(3), 14–17.

Handshape Closed 3 (page 42)

. . . a horse painting?

- Carroll, C. (1991). *Laurent Clerc.* Washington, DC: Kendall Green Publications.
- Debee, J.R. (1995). *Laurent Clerc, 1785–1869* [Videotape]. Pittsburgh, PA: DeBee Communications.
- Sonnenstrahl, D. (1996). De'VIA—What an odd word! (A historical perspective). In M. Garreston (Ed.), *Deafness: Historical perspectives—A deaf American monograph* (pp. 131–134). Silver Spring, MD: National Association of the Deaf.
- Sonnenstrahl, D. (2002). *Deaf artists in America: Colonial to contemporary.* San Diego, CA: DawnSignPress.

Handshape 3 (page 44)

. . . a rooster in a rocking chair?

- Groce, N. (1985). *Everyone here spoke sign language: Hereditary deafness on Martha's Vineyard.* Cambridge, MA: Harvard University Press.
- Listisard, M. (1997, May). Neon, sunflowers & double illusions: Betty Miller continues to grow as an artist and advocate. *Deaf Life*, 9(11), 22–29, 31–32.
- Schein, J., & Stewart, D. (1995). *Language in motion: Exploring the nature of sign.* Washington, DC: Gallaudet University Press.

Handshape Bent 3 (page 45)

. . . a bug winning a championship?

- Barber, A. (2003, Summer). U.S. shines in the land of the midnight sun. CSD *Spectrum*, 3(2), 40–45.
- Barish, J., & Barish, J. 19th *Summer Deaflympics: Rome 2001.* Silver Spring, MD: Webbynation.
- Jordan, J. (1996). *Comité international des sports des sourds.* In Garretson (Ed.), *Deafness: Historical*

perspectives—A deaf American monograph (pp. 57–59). Silver Spring, MD: National Association of the Deaf.

Handshape Bent L (page 46)

. . . a moon working as a relay operator?

- Around the country and beyond. (2003, July-September). *The GA-SK TDI's Quarterly News-Magazine*, 34,(3), 28–31.
- Video relay services at a glance. (2003, April-June). *The GA-SK TDI's Quarterly News-Magazine*, Vol. 34(2), 20–23.

Handshape L (page 48)

. . . a hair dryer welding?

- Branson, J., & Miller, D. (2002). *Damned for the difference*: T*he cultural construction of deaf people as disabled*. Washington, DC: Gallaudet University Press.
- Winefield, R. (1987). *Never the twain shall meet*: T*he communications debate*. Washington, DC: Gallaudet University Press.

Handshape I-L or I-L-Y (page 50)

..two airplanes falling in love?

- Emmorey, K. (2002). *Language, cognition, and the brain*: *Insights from sign language research*. Mahwah, NJ: Lawrence Erlbaum.
- Gallaudet, E. (1983). *History of the college for the deaf 1857–1907*. Washington, DC: Gallaudet College Press.

- Schein, J., & Stewart, D. (1995). *Language in motion*: *Exploring the nature of sign*. Washington, DC: Gallaudet University Press.

Handshape Y (page 51)

. . . a calf being shaved?

- Sheeks, E. (1994, March 25). Student congress meets again after inclement weather delays. *The Buff and Blue*, p. 1.

Handshape I–1 (page 52)

. . . a hippo mocking kids?

- James, L. (1998). ABC *stories* [Videotape]. Toronto, Ontario, Canada: Canadian Cultural Society of the Deaf.
- Moore, M., & Levitan, L. (1998, September). "Shoot for the moon:" Our YLC adventure. *Deaf Life*: *Special YLC Issue*, pp. 10–25.
- Rutherford, S. (1993). A *study of American deaf folklore*. Burtonsville, MD: Linstok Press.

- Tennant, R., & Brown, M. (1998). T*he American Sign Language handshape dictionary*. Washington, DC: Gallaudet University Press.

Handshape I (page 54)

. . . a rhino walking in high heels to a Deaf school?

- Johnston, E. (1997). Residential schools offer students deaf culture. *Perspectives in Education and Deafness*, 16(2), 4–5, 24.
- Reay, E. (1959, October). History of the Idaho School for the Deaf and the Blind. *The optimist*. Gooding, ID: Idaho School for the Deaf and the Blind.

- Van Cleve, J., & Crouch, B. (1990). A *place of their own*: *Creating the deaf community in America*. Washington, DC: Gallaudet University Press.

Handshape Modified 8 (page 56)

. . . a heart asking, "What's up?"

- Bahan, B.J. (1996). *Non-manual realization of agreement in American Sign Language.* Unpublished doctoral dissertation, Boston University, Boston.
- Bragg, B., & Bergman, E. (1981). *Tales from a club-room.* Washington, DC: Gallaudet College Press.
- DeBee, J.R. (1993). *The Los Angeles club of the deaf story* [Videotape]. Pittsburgh, PA: DeBee Communications.

Handshape 8 (page 58)

. . . meat telling a story?

- Andrews, J.F. (2001). *Mystery of the totems.* Salem, OR: Butte Publications.
- Bahan, B.J. (1992). American Sign Language literature: Inside the story. *Conference proceedings of Deaf studies: What's up?* (pp. 153–164). Washington, DC: Gallaudet University College for Continuing Education.
- Byrne, A. (1996). ASL storytelling to deaf children: "More! More! More!" In D.L. Smith & A.R. Small (Eds.), *Teacher research in a bilingual/bicultural school for deaf students* (pp. 49–62). Ontario, Canada: Ontario Ministry of Education and Training.
- Lentz, E., Mikos, K., & Smith, C. (1995). *The treasure: Poems by Ella Mae Lentz* [Videotape]. Hayward, CA: In Motion Press.
- Luczak, R. (2003). *Manny ASL: Stories in American Sign Language* [Videotape]. New York: ASL Storytelling.
- Peters, C.L. (2000). *Deaf American literature: From carnival to the canon.* Washington, DC: Gallaudet University Press.
- Rayman, J. (1999). Storytelling in the visual mode: A comparison of ASL and English. In E. Winston (Ed.), *Storytelling and conversation discourse in deaf communities.* Washington, DC: Gallaudet University Press.
- Smith, A.K. (in press). *Deaf Cinderella* [DVD & Book]. Frederick, MD: ASL Rose.
- Smith, A.K. & Terro, D. (in press). *Deaf coach now* [DVD & Book]. Frederick, MD: ASL Rose.

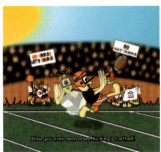

Handshape Open 8 (page 60)

. . . a bee kicking a football?

- French, J. (1988, Oct. 1) As eye see it. *Johnson's County Gazette,* pp. 5, 21.
- Johnson, J. (2002, October 20). ASD too much for Maryland. *The Daily Home,* p. B2.

Handshape K or P (page 61)

. . . a skunk babysitting King?

- Ammeson, J. (1996, April). High degree of success. *Northwest Airlines World Traveler,* 28(4), 66–68, 70–71.
- Carroll, C. (Ed.). (2002). *History through deaf eyes: Teacher's guide.* Washington, DC: Gallaudet University Laurent Clerc National Deaf Education Center.

Handshape R (page 62)

. . . a rocket wearing braids?

- Bullard, D. (1986). *Islay: A novel.* Silver Spring, MD: TJ Publishers.
- Jacobowitz, E.L. (1996). Deaf humor and positive political skills in communication. In V. Walters (Ed.), *Deaf studies IV: Visions of the past—Visions for the future* (pp. 97–109). Washington, DC: Gallaudet University College of Continuing Education.
- Ryan, S. (1991). *Planet way over yonder* [Videotape]. Washington, DC: Gallaudet University Department of Sign Communication.

Handshape W or 6 (page 64)

. . . a pea-brained $6 bill?

- Bahan, B. (1989). What If. . . Alexander Graham Bell had gotten his way? In S. Wilcox (Ed.), *American deaf culture* (pp. 83–87). Burtonsville, MD: Linstok Press.

- Lang, H. (2002). *A phone of our own: The deaf insurrection against ma bell.* Washington, DC: Gallaudet University Press.
- Winefield, R. (2000). *Never the twain shall meet: The communications debate* (3rd ed.). Washington, DC: Gallaudet University Press.

Handshape E (page 65)

. . . an En-DEAF-Quirer creating EEE sounds?

- Eastman, G. (1996). *Just a DEAF person's thoughts.* Burtonsville: MD: Sign Media.
- Lane, H. (1999). *The mask of benevolence: Disabling the deaf community.* San Diego, CA: DawnSignPress.
- Hoffmeister, R. (2000). A piece of the puzzle: ASL and reading comprehension in deaf children. In C. Chamberlain, J. Morford, & R. Mayberry (Eds.), *Language acquisition by eye* (pp. 143–163). Mahwah, NJ: Lawrence Erlbaum.
- Padden, C., & Ramsey, C. (1998). Reading ability in signing deaf children. *Topics in Language Disorders*, 18(4), 30–46.
- Prinz, P.M., & Strong, M. (1998). ASL proficiency and English literacy within a bilingual deaf education model of instruction. *Topics in Language Disorders*, 18(4), 47–60.
- Singleton, J.L., Morgan, D., DiGello, E., Wiles, J., & Rivers, R. (2004). Vocabulary use by low, moderate, and high ASL-proficient writers compared to hearing ESL and monolingual speakers. *Journal of Deaf Studies and Deaf Education*, 9(1), 86–103.
- Singleton, J., & Supalla, S. (1998). *The effects of ASL fluency upon deaf children's cognitive, linguistic, and social development.* Final report to the U.S. department of Education: Office of Special Education and Rehabilitation Services. Funded grant project (1993–1996). Unpublished manuscript, University of Illinois, Urbana-Champaign.
- Singleton, J.L., Supalla, S., Litchfield, S., & Schley, S. (1998). Modality constraints in ASL/English bilingual education. *Topics in Language Disorders*, 18 (4), 16–29.
- Wilbur, R.B. (2000). The use of ASL to support the development of English and literacy. *Journal of Deaf Studies and Deaf Education*, 5(1), 81–104.

About the Team that Created
Have You Ever Seen…? An American Sign Language (ASL) Handshape DVD/Book

Adonia K. Smith, *Author*

Adonia K. Smith, co-owner of ASL Rose, graduated from the Georgia School for the Deaf in 1988. She earned her bachelor's degree in Elementary Education (1995) and master's degree in Deaf Education (1996) from Gallaudet University. Upon graduation, she worked at the Alabama School for the Deaf as an elementary school teacher. She then went west to Texas where she taught graduate and undergraduate courses in the Deaf Education/Deaf Studies Department at Lamar University. She is currently a doctoral candidate, focusing on the development of a teacher-friendly American Sign Language assessment for deaf children. Today, Adonia utilizes multimedia technology in creating children's DVDs/books. This DVD/book is the first one of the series that she and Dr. E. Lynn Jacobowitz, co-owners of ASL Rose are creating. Adonia, Charm, her Deaf Border Collie, and Amber, her Hearing Aussie Shepard, make their home in Woodbine, Maryland.

E. Lynn Jacobowitz, *Author*

E. Lynn Jacobowitz, Ph.D., co-owner of ASL Rose, is an associate professor in the Department of American Sign Language and Deaf Studies at Gallaudet University. She holds a professional American Sign Language Teachers Association (ASLTA) certification and was ASLTA president from 1995 to 1998. Dr. Jacobowitz was past Chair of the National ASLTA ASL Curriculum Project and ASL Legislation. She has given numerous workshops and presentations on ASL, Deaf culture, Deaf folklore, methods, and materials for sign language teachers. She is well-known for her comedy and storytelling performances, consultations, articles, and cartoons about Deaf culture and humor. Dr. Jacobowitz makes her home with her lifelong partner, Dr. Kathleen M. Wood and their daughters, Eve and Anna in Frederick, Maryland.

Tamara Davidson, *Illustrator*

Tamara Davidson earned her associate's degree in Applied Arts and Computer Graphics from the National Technical Institute of the Deaf at the Rochester Institute of Technology in 1988. Originally from Dayton, Ohio, Tamara has provided count-less illustrations and comics for several organizations and publications, including the Buckeye Girl Scouts Council, ME TOO! A Substance Abuse Prevention Project for Deaf Youth, WE TOO! A Resiliency Enhancement Project for Preschoolers with Special Needs, and SIG*News*. She works as a freelance illustrator and lives in Ypsilanti, Michigan with her husband and two cats.

James R. DeBee

James R. DeBee is the founder of DeBee Communications, Inc., that produces documentaries, commercials and educational videotapes. He holds two degrees in Radio, Television and Film from California State University, Northridge, California and in Media Communications Technology from Rochester Institute of Technology and National Technical Institute for the Deaf, Rochester, New York. He also has an M.S. in Educational Technology Management and Public Policy from Carnegie Mellon University, Pittsburgh, PA. Mr. DeBee has over twenty-five years of video/film experience with all technical aspects of video production. He has worked in many capacities such as producer, director, writer, editor, lighting director, photographer, media specialist, and executive producer. His partial credit list includes KTLA-5, Beyond Sound, Group W Cable, Silent Network, National Association of the Deaf, National Catholic Office for the Deaf, DawnSign Press/Pictures, PBS, Deaf West Theatre, KCET, GLAD, and Gallaudet University.

Rosa Lee Gallimore, *Cultural Vignettes*, ASL *Signer*

Born in Loma Linda, California, Rosa Lee Gallimore spent her childhood years living in Oregon with her two brothers. She was home-schooled by her mother until her family moved to Nebraska, where she was enrolled in a private mainstream school for a few years before entering the Indiana School for the Deaf. Rosa Lee began her artistic pursuit at the National Technical Institute for the Deaf, where she founded a performance group, D*angerous* S*igns*, and served as artistic director. After receiving a bachelor's degree in Social Work, Rosa returned to Oregon to pursue her master's degree in Rehabilitation Counseling. She continues to make her home in Oregon and works as a rehabilitation counselor, as well as the Executive Director of Liberty Road Productions.

ASL *Signers*

Carey Ballard is a first grader at the Maryland School for the Deaf in Frederick. His Deaf parents are Barbara ("Bo") and Rick Ballard.

Kassandra Ballard is a semi-CODA (hearing in one ear and deaf in the other) and the sister of Carey Ballard. She is a third grader at Spring Ridge Elementary in Frederick, Maryland.

Demi Bingham attends pre-kindergarten at the Maryland School for the Deaf in Frederick and has a deaf brother, Kyle. Her Deaf parents are Bonnie and James Bingham.

Ivana Corey-Genievsky is a third grader at the Maryland School for the Deaf in Frederick. Her Deaf parents are Rita Corey and Alex Genievsky.

Payne Frankowiak is in the Family Education Program at the Maryland School for the Deaf in Frederick. She has a deaf sister, Hilary, and Deaf parents, Stacia and Joe Frankowiak.

Sayre Huddleston is in kindergarten at the Maryland School for the Deaf in Frederick. He has an older Deaf sister, a CODA sister, and Deaf parents, Susie and Tom Huddleston.

Karita Lewis has two deaf siblings, Marika and Rory. She is a pre-kindergarten student at the Maryland School for the Deaf in Frederick. Her Deaf parents are Robert and Risa Lewis.

Niko Lutes-Stein is a pre-kindergartener at the Texas School for the Deaf in Austin. His adoptive parents are Jeff Lutes (hearing) and Gary Stein (Deaf).

Alton Jake ("AJ") Markel is a third grader at the Maryland School for the Deaf in Frederick. His family includes a Deaf younger sister, Dabitha ("DJ"), Deaf mother, Jennifer Markel-Woomer, and Deaf stepfather, Eric Woomer.

Emmanuel Perrodin-Njoku is a first grader at the Kendall Demonstration Elementary School in Washington, DC. His Deaf parents are Brenda Perrodin and Philip Obi Njoku.

Hakeem Schiller is a first grader at the Maryland School for the Deaf in Frederick. His parents, James and Donna Schiller, are hearing and use ASL. His sister, Maya (also hearing), communicates with her brother using ASL.

Alexa Simmons is in the first grade at the Maryland School for the Deaf in Frederick. Her parents, Alex and Jennifer Simmons, and her brother, Cody, are all Deaf.

Freya Seremeth is in the Family Education Program at the Maryland School for the Deaf in Frederick. Alphabetically, she is the last letter in her family: her oldest sister, Augusta; her father, Bobby; her older brother, Chaz; her mother, Dawn Schriver; and her youngest brother, Egan; are all Deaf.

Jamal Whitehurst is a CODA and a pre-kindergartner at Spring Ridge Elementary in Frederick, Maryland. Jamal has a Deaf baby brother, Jalen, and his parents are Jaron (hearing) and Julie Whitehurst (Deaf).

www.aslrose.com